Listening To The Pause

Finding Wisdom in an Unwanted Pause

Bhawna Sindhwani

BookLeaf Publishing

India | USA | UK

Made with ❤ on the BookLeaf Publishing Platform

www.bookleafpub.in

www.bookleafpub.com

Dedication

I dedicate this book first and foremost to both sides of my family and then to my doctors and caregivers. During my recovery from an unexpected medical incident, my family stood by me, offering unwavering emotional and physical support. To those who made the past few months all about me, allowing me to stand on my feet again—quite literally—I realize just how fortunate I am to have each of you. The family members who took time out of their busy lives to visit me brought me not just care but a sense of deep mental anchoring.

I also dedicate this to the doctors, nurses, and caregivers (cook, wheelchair operator, cleaner) who provided both expertise and compassion. Your dedication not only healed my body but also gave me the strength to believe in recovery. You turned moments of uncertainty into hope, and for that, I am eternally grateful.

I am forever grateful to you all!

Preface

This collection began in the quiet shadows of a difficult time.

When I first put pen to paper—well, my phone and finger, because let's be honest, most of this was typed while lying flat with one eye open—I was grappling with the weight of an unexpected medical diagnosis. It reshaped my days, my thoughts, and occasionally my ability to remember what day it even was. The early poems reflect that rawness. They are honest, vulnerable, and at times, unapologetically moody. Writing them wasn't just creative—it was survival. A way to say, "This is hard," without needing a response.

But healing, I've learned, isn't a straight line. Somewhere between the appointments, the naps, and the very questionable patient food, I started to laugh again. Not always at the right moments, but laughter showed up anyway—usually right after a meltdown or a bad pun. And once it returned, so did a lighter voice in my writing.

As you turn the pages of this collection, you'll walk with me from the heavy to the humorous, from the aching to the absurd. The poems shift gradually, tracing the slow but steady rhythm of healing—and the unexpected joy of finding yourself again, even when things are still a little messy.

If you're in a tough season, I hope these words offer
some comfort, and maybe even a smile. If you're in a
good place, may they remind you how strong we really
are when things fall apart—and how helpful a bit of
humor can be in putting them back together.

With warmth,
Bhawna

Acknowledgements

I wrote these poems during a period when I was nearly bedridden. What began as a vacation turned into a medical nightmare, requiring leg surgery that confined me to bed for a month, followed by slow, gradual movements in the second month and the use of a walking stick in the third month. This unexpected pause in my otherwise busy life gave me a chance to witness the world passively, including my own thoughts and emotions. In this stillness, I began reflecting and recording my thoughts with a touch of aesthetics—adding rhyming words—and thus, this collection was born.

Much like my physical recovery, these poems unfold through distinct stages. They start with a sense of heaviness and inertia, mirroring the days spent bedridden. Slowly, they find a steadier rhythm, reflecting the cautious but hopeful steps taken with support. Finally, they reach a place of lightness and freedom, much like the moment I stood on my own again. The emotional journey—of stillness, struggle, strength, and uplift—is what I hope to convey through these words. I hope you find meaning and enjoyment in this collection, just as I found healing in its creation.

1. The Silence Between Us

So many words I left unspoken,
So many truths began to waken.
Did I choose the right thing, when I stood still,
When you chased echoes over the hill?

The roads you wandered, vast and wild,
Called to the dreamer, the restless child.
I watched you go; I let you be-
Was that mercy or cruelty?

So many words I left untold,
So many truths began to unfold.
Did I choose right when I chose to stay?
While you wandered so far away?

The roads you walked were wild and free,
A path unknown, not meant for me,
Yet in my heart, the question remains,
Did silence spare us or bring us pain?

The trails you followed, open and untamed,
Becokned the dreamer, the one unchained.
I let you go; I held my peace-
Was that compassion, or a quiet release?

Did silence shield us from the storm?

Or was it the fire that kept us warm?

I ask myself again, as echoes fade in twilight's glow,

In all we lost, in all we gained,

Were we freed, or just restrained?

2. Echoes of the Final Yuga

Everyone is busy; yet empty inside,
Smiling for show, where can truth reside?
Praises snug in a hollow tune.
Each heart craving to outshine the moon.

What is this world, where silence screams,
Where love is lost in selfish dreams?
Hands that once lifted, now push away,
souls forgotten in the rush of the day.

Is this Kalyuga, where light decays,
Where virtue crumbles and falsehood sways?
Where kindness is weakness, truth is denied,
 And power is worshipped, though hollow inside?

But beneath the ruin, embers still glow,
Buried in hearts too weary to show.
Can we unearth what time betrayed,
Or are we shadows, slowly unmade?

3. The Sacred Vessel

The body is an instrument, glowing with light,
Yet we forget what keeps it right.
We chase the world, its fleeting highs,
Only to learn they're veiled lies.

Money, a mansion, a paycheck grand,
Seem to offer a life well-planned.
But there are dreams that make us blind,
Feeding the ego, caging the mind.

The second-last truth-—this body divine,
A temple of life, sacred, sublime.
Yet beyond it lies the final key.
The soul is eternal, boundless, and free!

4. The Vanished Cheer

Everyone needs a cheerleader; that's true,
Once, that was you—so steady, so blue.
You lifted me high, my anchor, my light,
Now all I find is an empty night.

You were my strength, my greatest gain,
Now all I feel is your cold disdain.
Was it the miles, the weight of time?
Did love erode, like words in rhyme?

A believer, a dreamer, voice so near,
Gone in a whisper, lost in the sphere.
Was it my flaws, my wrong decisions?
Or did you drift without a reason?

You are missed, your cheer now gone,
Like a melody lost at the break of dawn.
All I seek is a soul sincere.
A hand to hold, a heart kept near.

5. The Fire Within

Not wise enough, not seasoned yet,
But I hold a fire you won't forget,
Is it money, or is it fame?
Or the rush of oxytocin in the game?

With dopamine dreams and serotonin highs,
I chase my goals with fearless eyes.
Cortisol creeps when failures appear,
But I turn that stress into fuel, not fear.
Adrenaline surges, passion ignites,
Euphoria peaks on sleepless nights.

Cutting corners, jumping high,
Turning hurdles into my sky.
Endorphins rise as I push through pain,
Each setback only sharpens my aim.
Anticipation tingles; my heart beats fast,
Every risk is a thrill that's built to last.

The second rise—no biggest cheers,
No leaders near to calm my fears.
The next try's weight is hard to bear,
Yet I push through, fierce and rare.

No chorus chants my name this time,
No guiding hands, no safety lines.
The ones I love, the ones I trust,
Now question if my dreams are just.
Their faith is faint; their doubt runs deep,
Their whispers steal the strength I keep.
Cortisol spikes, anxiety calls,
Yet I refuse to let it stall
The fire within, the spark so bright,
I rise once more; I win this fight.

No guarantee of a triumphant fate,
No certainty that success awaits.
Perhaps the climb will yield no crown,
Perhaps I'll stumble, crash back down.
But when my hair turns silver-white,
And memories gleam in softer light,
Regret will never cloud my mind,
I pursued, I sought, I climbed.

No fear, no pause, just pure devotion,
Fueled by fire and raw emotion.
Dopamine soars as I dare once more,
Stronger than ever, ready to soar!

6. The Boastful Brick

Each brick in the fortress, chest puffed with pride,
Believes it's the reason the walls stand wide.
It scoffs at the mortar, unseen in the seams,
Dismissing the glue that binds all its dreams.

"I am the backbone! The weight I endure!
No other brick is as strong or as pure!
Without me, this structure would falter and break,
No stone, no bond, could dare to partake!"

Oh, how it boasts in it's rigid disguise,
Blind to the cracks that whisper its lies.
It mocks the cement with a pompous display,
Forgetting its form is just molded decsy.

Does the brick now know? Has it not seen?
Alone, it's nothing but dust in between.
A hardened lump, so brittle and frail,
No foundation, no function—just destined to fail.

Yet it struts, convinced it's divine,
That every arch and tower is solely its spine.
It dreams itself marble; it calls itself gold,
Yet it's nothing but earth—just dirt that's cold.

For if the bond were to loosen and slip,
The brick would tumble, betrayed by its grip.
Once so haughty, now shattered and torn,
A lesson in pride, abandoned, forlorn.

So let the brick learn, before it's too late,
That strength isn't found in a singular fate.
For power is shared, not hoarded in vain-
A wall without union is dust in the rain.

7. A Reckoning of Neglect

No fire, no force, no discipline in sight,
You drift like a ghost through the weight of the night.
What makes you so sure you've got it all right?
Or is it just arrogance shrouded in spite?

A life without structure - chaos untamed,
No rhythm, no lessons, no path to be named.
Two souls in your hands, yet you squander their fate
Letting time slip as you reason too late.

No doors to the world, no whispers pf lore,
No glimpses of culture, no keys to the door.
What will they be but reflection of shame,
Lost in the dark, with no one to blame?

Not a teacher, not a guide, not a partner of worth,
What mockery, what madness, to claim you know earth!
Parading your wisdom, a hollow disguise—yet blind to
the ruin you craft with your lies.

8. A Fool, They Whisper

He dwells within a shadowed sphere,
A cocoon of thought, both far and near.
They mock his ways; they call him blind.
Yet in the silence, truth unwinds.

A fool, they whisper-—just a chance.
Yet fate was shaped by careful dance.
His youth was lots, or so they claim,
But every ember built his flame.

They see the gold, the fleeting prize,
Yet miss the light behind his eyes.
They see the triumph, bold and grand,
But not the ghosts that hold his hand.

He loved the lost, or so they say.
Or walked where restless spirits stray.
But truth is twisted, veiled in night,
What gleams outside may lack true light.

His offspring deny, his guardians fade,
His better half turns love to shade.
Yet still, he runs, through storm and tide,
Chasing whispers the world denied.

But what is the prize for all he has gained?
Fame without faces, wealth with no name.
The echoes grow louder, the silence more deep-—is he
awake or lost in his sleep?

A kingdom of whispers, a throne of regret,
A past he outran but cannot forget.
The stars in his grasp feel colder than stone.
For what is a crown when worn all alone?

9. Imposed Fate

Ever since you chose your way,
I watched the seasons fade to grey.
A web of lies, so neatly spun,
Turned to malice, one by one.

Right or wrong - it mattered none.
The choice was forced; the deed was done.
You held a gift so deftly spun,
A perfect trick—I was the one.

I fell for whispers, soft yet cruel,
Helpless, shattered, torn apart,
Injustice burned within my heart,
And now I walk with endless scars.

Step by step, the weight grew tall,
Yet I stood silent through it all.
I could have warned; I could have tried.
Instead, I let the truth subside.

It wasn't just me who felt the fall,
Another suffered through it all.
You closed your eyes till dusk drew near,
Ignoring every silent tear.

Now you see what you have done,
But fate won't let you clock rerun.
No turning back, no bridge to mend,
Just echoes stretching to the end.

All that you feared, all that you disdained,
Now lingers in the life you've gained.
The wisdom lost, the price so steep,
Regret the only truth you keep.

For love is truth, and truth was lost,
And now we bear the aching cost.
Not just of you, but all we knew-
A life unspoken, painted blue.

10. O Childhood, Dear

The purest form, so light, so bright,
A treasure gleaming in golden light.
No fears to chase, no debts to pay,
Just endless dreams and games to play.

Oh, childhood dear, so wild, so true.
A fleeting breeze in skies so blue.
You come and go like winds that glide,
Unseen until adulthood cried.

You shade me soft in parents' embrace,
A sky of love, a warm, safe place.
Siblings soaring, wild and high,
Like birds that own the endless sky.

Diwali/Christmas glows in memory's chest,
A bank of moments, the very best.
No fear, no plans, just games to crack.
A perfect world with no looking back!

The tantrums, the toys, the sweet little joys,
The monsters to beat, the love to enjoy.
A mom so dear, a dad so bold,
A story of heroes, forever told.

Can you return? Oh, tell me true!
"Yes! says childhood, "I come in three hues-
Once as yourself, wild and bright,
Twice through your child, a pure delight,
Thrice when you're old, with eyes so wise,
A child once more in life's disguise."

Oh childhood dear, you never fade,
Forever alive in the hearts you've made!

11. Life in Full Circle

We leave our homes with hearts so light,
Chasing dreams in morning's bright.
A nest we build with hands alone,
No parents' feathers—just our own.

The start is fierce, a hurried race,
Each step a dance, each turn a chase.
Midway glows with triumph's gleam,
But fades into a lonesome dream.

We hit mid-age, we pause, we sigh,
Thinking our childhood was caged and dry.
Only to find, through time's confessing,
We long once more for parents' blessing.

You wish to return, to mend, to stay,
But life has led you far away.
You built a house so grand, so tall,
Yet miss the warmth that made it all.

Behind, our childhood drifts away,
Parents watching, hopes at bay.
We build anew, so proud, so free,
Yet time reveals its irony.

For when our children take their flight,
We stand where once our parents might.
Regret and love, a woven thread,
A circle spun by words unsaid.

12. The Eternal Flame

O Soul, the silent, sacred all,
The cosmic breath, the mystic call—
You are the center, pure and whole,
A spark divine, the dreamer's soul.

A gleam of Light in mortal frame,
Yet far beyond the flesh or name.
A universe within you glows,
Untouched by time, untouched by woes.

Child of the Supreme, O radiant flame,
Infinite power, beyond all name.
You wear the body like a robe,
Then cast it off to roam the globe.

From birth to birth, through endless skies,
You travel on where karma lies.
Each deed a thread, each choice a seed,
Woven in the web of need.

But humans fall to pride and lore,
They chase the dust and ask for more.
Blinded by gold, by name and fame,
They lose the self, forget the flame.

The body's cloth—just threads and skin,
It wears, it tears, it sheds again.
The wise don't mourn its fleeting stay—
They rise, they shine, they find the Way.

For truth is this: we are not clay,
But light that never fades away.
To live awakened, full and free—
Is to know, at last, eternity.

13. To My Daughter...

Daughters are the precious dream,
A blessing from the stars, it seems,
A gift bestowed from realms above,
Wrapped in innocence and love.

She is the mother, kind and true,
A sister's heart, so pure, so new,
A friend to laugh and gently mend,
A soul whose light will never end.

Her care, a gentle breeze at dawn,
Her wisdom flows, a river drawn.
She plays with joy, her spirit free,
A miracle, a part of me.

With every step, her heart does sail,
Through life, with grace, she will prevail.
My pride, my joy, my deepest light,
She makes the world feel warm and bright.

For in my daughter, I see the world,
A dream, a love, unfurled,
A gift divine, a treasure grand,
Forever holding my heart in her hand.

14. Fork You, Feelings

Food, oh food—why are you so kind,
Tempting both body and troubled mind?
Even when hunger dares not call,
You rise to meet me, feeding all.

Joy, sorrow, silence, or ache,
You're the comfort I quickly take.
I kiss you deeply with every bite,
Searching for warmth in the absence of light.

Each problem shrinks when you arrive,
On glowing screens, you come alive.
Not books, not people, none compete—
You're the friend I turn to eat.

My eyes drink deep your sugared grace,
Your scent invades my sacred space.
My mouth becomes a greedy stream,
As my soul devours a fleeting dream.

But soon, the spell begins to fade,
My stomach speaks the truth I evade:
There was no joy inside that loot,
No healing in that silent pursuit.

You promised peace; you wore disguise,
But left me numb beneath the lies.
The heart still weeps, the soul still aches,
The body bends with all it takes.

You are a friend, but only in part—
A tender thief of the wounded heart.
A whisper says, "Just one more bite."
But wholeness lives in choosing light.

15. In Her Embrace, I Become

Rigid as rock,
Yet gentle as glow.

Fierce as fire,
Yet calm as snow.

Sharp as spines,
Yet tender as thyme.

Tough as iron,
Yet soft as chimes.

Strict as stick,
Yet brave beneath.

Angry a lot,
Yet eyes damp as dew.

Irritable easy,
Yet insightful breezy.

Coarse as beach sand,
Compassionate as grand.

Wild as winds,
Yet rooted as roots.

Hardened as stone,
Yet blooming as shoots.

You are a blend of extremes,
Like sunlit days and moonlit dreams.

A fierce force and a soft embrace,
A balance of power, grace, and space.

That's my mother,
Now I am you.

16. On Your Special Day

On this special day, I wish you joy,
A heart full of love, no sorrow, no ploy.
You are a treasure, a guiding light,
In your warmth, my world feels right.

Your love and care have shaped my way,
Guiding me through both night and day.
Not just a guiding light, but a friend so true,
A beautiful soul in all that you do.

From your patience, I learn to be still,
To face life's storms with unwavering will.
In your calm, I find strength to grow,
With every lesson, my spirit flows.

Your presence makes my life more bright,
With your love, I find endless delight.
Forever grateful for the love you share,
In your embrace, I feel love's pure air.

May happiness and health be yours each year,
With every blessing, may your heart stay clear.
I love you dearly, with all my might,
In you, I find love as pure as light.

17. Clock in at 9

Is it a routine, or a clever old lie?
To trap us all 'til the day we die?
We rise, we grind, we sip burnt brew,
And wonder what we were meant to do.

Sure, it pays for bills and hilltop stays,
Where we scroll emails through holidays.
It funds our houses, cars with flair,
Though we barely have time to sit in a chair.

No yoga, no art, no time for Zen,
No deep convos with family or friends.
Our souls are tired, our backs are sore,
But hey! Look—our savings grew a little more!

I paused and asked, mid spreadsheet stare,
"If not this job... then what? And where?"
Could I be a painter? A poet? A knight?
But truth be told—I fear stage fright.

So back to the grind, I sip my tea,
And fake a smile professionally.
Till I write a hit or start a spree,
Or launch a startup selling ghee.

Until a plan divine aligns,
I'll keep showing up—clock in at nine! ;)

18. Nowhere Belong

Love the food at home—spicy delight,
But abroad, my stomach sleeps at night.
Between bloating joy and salads too long—
I'm not confused, I just nowhere belong.

Love the hustle and aunties who pry,
But abroad no one even bats an eye.
One place's gossip, another's a blog—
I'm not confused, I just nowhere belong.

Love the lights and wedding drums,
But also love peace (and no uninvited chums).
One's loud joy, the other's quiet song—
I'm not confused, I just nowhere belong.

"Come back soon," Mom had said,
Now her WhatsApp texts fill me with dread.
She sends me recipes, prayers, and memes,
While I chase jobs and half-baked dreams.
Between homesick nights and moving on,
Did I lose the place I once leaned upon?
I'm not confused, I just nowhere belong.

It's not identity, nor mid-life haze,

Though I do forget what month it says.
I've seen too much, worn too many shoes—
Some call it growth, I call it confused.
I'm not lost, but I'm tagging along—
I'm not confused, I just nowhere belong.

Maybe I want too much on my plate—
Chole bhature with lassi that's great,
Momos with friends, laughter on replay,
But also deep talks in a quiet café.
Between greasy hands and clinking glasses' song—
I'm not confused, I just nowhere belong.

Oh wait... maybe I'm just greedy all along.
Or maybe I just want a home where snacks last long.
Where siblings tease and parents care,
And I don't have to choose where I belong...

19. 40, 40, are You Naughty?

40, 40, are you naughty?
Do you make life carefree, or just kinda spotty?
Will there be no stress and endless party?
Can I still dance all night without feeling too farty?

You'll let my hair down, make me a hottie,
Oh, I can't wait to be sassy and frosty!

But wait, what's this? The late 30's are here,
Back aches, frozen shoulder, and a stash of fear.
Can't digest like before, and acid's my new mate,
Trying to stretch without feeling like I'm at a broken
state.

40 promised fun, wild days ahead,
Wealth and success, a life well-fed.
But now I'm Googling "How to sleep without pain,"
And "How to get rid of this constant brain drain."

Lifestyle changes were supposed to be chic,
But it's more about "Don't eat that, you'll be sick!"
I was meant to be fit, healthy, and rich,
But now I'm just searching for a cure for this itch.

I thought I'd be sipping champagne, carefree and spry,
But here I am, wishing my knees wouldn't sigh.
A life of luxury, cocktails in hand,
Instead, I'm just trying to find my old tan.

And those clicking bones? Don't get me started,
I move and they snap, crackle, pop—I'm mildly faint-
hearted.
It's like a symphony of joints, each time I rise,
I sound like a Rice Krispies treat that's in disguise.

But, hey, this is what it is, I won't cry,
It's the spirit and health that will get me by.
So here's to the 40's, the smoothest of rides,
With a little back pain and a lot of pride!

20. The Matcha Meltdown (A Love Story in Sips)

All I crave is a cup of green—
Not money, not fame—just caffeine!
But not just any tea, oh no, don't play—
It's matcha, the queen of my day.

She arrives like royalty in a humble cup,
I bow, I whisper, "Girl, what's up?"
I take one sip—my toes go numb,
My spine does jazz hands, my brain says, "YUM!"

My food pipe—oh bless that slide,
Throws a party from the inside.
My stomach? She weeps, "We are reborn!"
Then does a slow-mo cartwheel at dawn.

With each green gulp, I start to sway,
My kneecaps leave—they float away.
My liver hums a lullaby,
My spleen moonwalks, I don't know why.

I'm melting like butter in a Netflix scene,
Dramatic gasp—Is this what peace means?
One more sip—BOOM! My chakras align.

I suddenly remember my Netflix PIN and a past life as a
samurai.

Matcha doesn't just energize—
It gently slaps me 'til I'm wise.
It unclogs my soul, unghosts my ex,
Organizes my files, sends helpful texts.

To the tea master who first whisked this brew,
May your eyebrows always stay on fleek and true.
May your froth rise high and your leaves stay bold,
You're the MVP in green and gold.

So next time you sip, don't just drink—
Feel your pancreas do a wink.
It's not just tea. It's a full-body spa.
Matcha, my love... ooh la la!

21. Gratitude in Verse (A farewell to the 21-day poem challenge)

This marks the close of my poetic spree,
Twenty-one days of setting my thoughts free.
I thought, I felt, I wrestled and grew,
Each line a mirror, each word a clue.

I wrote what life dared to unfold,
Stories in whispers, brave and bold.
I smiled, I wept, I stumbled, I soared,
Regret tapped lightly, but truth was restored.

A roller coaster—I held on tight,
With verses born in day and night.
I don't know if you'll relate or see,
The heart I poured in poetry.

I don't know if it will rise or fall,
Or earn your silence, praise, or call.
But know this came from a sacred place,
Unfiltered truth I chose to face.

No mask, no gloss, no imitation—

Just raw and real, with inspiration.
No mutations in the feeling flow,
Only the light I came to know.

So here I stand, my spirit high,
With humbled heart and tear-kissed eye.
Thank you for walking beside my way—
For reading, feeling, or choosing to stay.